C-SUITE BOUND

C-Suite Bound

How Self-Discovery Leads to Ultimate Success

Veronica Villarreal

Published by Game Changer Publishing

Paperback ISBN: 978-1-965653-88-3
Hardcover ISBN: 978-1-965653-30-2
Digital ISBN: 978-1-965653-31-9

www.GameChangerPublishing.com

DEDICATION

To all who have guided me on this career journey.

To all who have granted me opportunities that most minority women are not afforded at such a young age.

To all who have supported my crazy ideas and have been by my side riding this amazing wave called life.

To all who have learned to appreciate and love my true heart and soul.

To the people who have supported me with their unconditional love.

To the one lady that I get to call my mom, my best friend, my mentor, and my biggest supporter.

Read This First

For inquiries or mentorship opportunities,
feel free to connect with me on LinkedIn.

Scan the QR Code Here:

C-Suite Bound

How Self-Discovery Leads to Ultimate Success

Veronica Villarreal

GC GAME CHANGER
PUBLISHING

www.GameChangerPublishing.com

Table of Contents

Introduction 1

Chapter 1 – Molding Your Career Journey.................................3

Chapter 2 – Focus on Your Purpose in Life 15

Chapter 3 – Leading Multigenerational Teams 23

Chapter 4 – Always Be Yourself 35

Chapter 5 – Say YES to Everything 49

Chapter 6 – Success Is Not Achieved Without Support 61

Chapter 7 – You Have to Fail to Succeed 73

Chapter 8 – Stop Doubting Yourself..85

Chapter 9 – The Reality of Being in the C-Suite at Age 30 95

Introduction

Some leaders will tell you everything they do right, but most are not as vulnerable to sharing what they do wrong. And that, I believe, is a big mistake when you want to help others grow. I've been fortunate to have opportunities in my life to get me to the C-suite at 30. Now, I tend to reflect on what I could have done better and what I still need to work on. If I can move up by not being the smartest, the prettiest, or the most polished, then I believe anyone can do it with just the right mindset. There are many resources out there that teach leadership skills, goals, self-reflection, and behavioral traits to work on so that you may be successful. Having the mindset of being a lifelong learner, opening your mind to different views of life, and knowing that there is always something new to learn will help you be ahead of most of your peers.

Every chapter of this book will shed some light on the mistakes I made, the ones I have seen others make, or the ones my colleagues have experienced. If you make a mistake, own it, fix it, and tell others so they won't make the same ones. As leaders, you do not want others to recreate the wheel unless the wheel is flat or broken.

People will try to imitate you if they look up to you or hate you, even if they have never had a cup of coffee with you—and that is okay. You are here in this world for a reason, and only you know what steps you have to take to get the most out of your experience in life. To stay focused on my career journey and not get stuck in funks, I have picked up the following values along the way:

1. Know that every experience and decision, whether good or bad, will mold your career journey.

2. Always circle back to your purpose in life to be able to either get out of your funk or change direction.

3. Don't listen to white noise or be influenced by societal norms to fit a mold in which you will most likely be miserable.

4. Learn to say yes to everything you can without sacrificing your well-being and your superior's work deadlines.

5. Have the mindset to empower others without your insecurities getting in the way.

6. Know that every failure is a lesson learned.

7. Have the confidence to never underestimate your worth and what you bring to the table.

8. Be able to get out of your head and adjust to different personalities, mindsets, and generational stigmas.

9. Know the responsibility of holding a title and how you plan to use it for good.

CHAPTER 1

Molding Your Career Journey

It has taken me a while to realize who Veronica really is and not who society wants Veronica to be. I like to describe myself as a "Millennial Latina Leader" who is constantly trying to enhance other people's strengths so they can do better. I want careerists at any age to know we are all going through struggles, and it is okay. There are many paths to take to get to your career goals, but you definitely need to seek guidance along the way to learn from others' experiences and understand the sacrifices and responsibilities that come with that career choice. There are decisions that you have to make to get you to where you want to be in your career journey, and it is never too late to pivot.

Culture

Being raised in a predominantly Hispanic town where our cultural values were instilled in us very early on, I did not realize how much I lived in a Mexican *burbuja* (bubble). I thought education was important, but according to societal norms, it was not as important as getting married at a certain age and raising a family. As I got older and was surrounded by strong single women sacrificing their dreams and desires to take care of others, I realized I could make an impact, but I didn't know how and what that would be.

In our Mexican culture, hospitality—through feeding everyone who comes through our door—is a way we show people our love. We want everyone to enjoy their time when we are together, sharing stories, laughter, and sometimes singing and dancing; not always in the same order, but sometimes all at the same time. Being a Mexican-American has always been a challenge, trying to fit into what society wanted me to be. My family that lived in Mexico would correct my "Spanglish" when I spoke to them, and our family and friends in America would correct or giggle when I spoke English with my Mexican accent, as Spanish was my first language until elementary school. I have learned to love who I really am and laugh at myself when I run out of English words to say *y una palabra extragenera se me pasa de la lengua* (and a strange word slips off my tongue).

Life Mentors

There are many women and men in my life that I have looked up to for various reasons, but the top two have been my mother and my late aunt. These women are extremely different but share the same characteristics of being a servant and unconventional leaders in their roles in life.

My mom's entire life was devoted to providing for my sister and me after my father passed away when I was one and my sister was three years old. Her selflessness in finding a job to support us had to kick into gear, whether she liked it or not. My mom was dedicated and extremely loyal to her job so that she could provide for us. Her purpose in life was to raise us to be independent human beings who did not have to depend on someone else to take care of us. This really shaped me into wanting to serve others in the same way she'd sacrificed herself to serve us. She is now happily married after 34 years of being a widower, which makes me believe you can find love at any age with the right mindset.

My aunt became an influential teacher at 19 and retired after 48 years of service. My sister and I always admired how independent she was. She never got married and had kids of her own. She told us stories of how she used to go to work and then come home and work at my grandma and grandpa's grocery store before they closed it. It wasn't until my aunt passed that I understood how much she gave back to her students. She was awarded Teacher of The Year for the State of Texas for her dedication to others. When I started working, she gave us career advice every chance she got by telling us stories about her and her coworkers' experiences. I never thought I would experience the same issues until I realized it doesn't matter what field you are in: navigating work politics, including nepotism and favoritism; building beautiful, lasting friendships at work; being envied for being praised as a hard worker by coworkers who didn't work as hard; and loving and seeing the impact you have made on others' lives—like my aunt with her students and myself with the people I interact with at work. We are all human with diverse personalities.

Study Abroad Programs

When I turned 21, I was accepted to study abroad in Morocco. I didn't tell anyone I had applied until I was accepted and figured out how I would pay for it. I had never been abroad and had never applied for a passport as I didn't need one to cross into Mexico (Now you need a passport to cross the border). I still remember the smell of the Sahara Desert, where my classmates and I spent the night under the dark sky, just connecting with nature and all its sounds. When speaking to the guides who set up the tents and cooked our dinner, I realized how little I knew about this world and what true inner peace actually meant. These men spoke their native tongue and some other languages they had picked up from tourists. They were immensely happy, and you could feel that in their presence.

I loved Morocco because of the many beautiful experiences I had to touch, feel, smell, and taste different things, but also how much the country humbled me. I returned home and started reevaluating my superficial friendships, my relationship with a higher being, and how I would fulfill my purpose in life. I started seeing things in a different way and noticing how people complained about first-world problems when they had never experienced third-world situations. Now, when I get the chance to speak to students, I highly encourage them to experience a study abroad program. It completely changed my tunnel-vision way of thinking.

Lifelong Learning

When we are young, we feel like we know everything about the world and where we think we should be in our lives. I always tell people you only know what you know. There is an entire universe we can never comprehend, which is okay. What is not okay is to leave college, land a job, and stop learning. I don't believe you need a degree to accomplish your dreams, but I do think it helps you get in the door when you have no experience and you aren't starting a business. Being a lifelong learner keeps you up to date with current trends and generational needs.

When you stop sharpening your skills and learning new skills, you stop being valuable or relevant to your employer or your customers if you are starting up a business. If you are in a career field you want to stay in, start looking for the best associations it has and start obtaining certifications. Certifications are especially important when you do not have the experience that others do. When I was completely new to my department in ambulatory operations, I started reading up on best practices and also signing up for the associations geared towards it. I wanted to learn as much as possible so I could have some sort of input instead of just absorbing knowledge from everyone else around me.

Employment or Self-Employment

I had always wanted to work in an organization where I could think on my own and grow there without the responsibility of having to worry about someone else's livelihood. Many people struggle with wanting to own their own business instead of working a nine-to-five job. There is no right or wrong answer to your decision, but if you do not decide and want to do both things, it could be more challenging. When I was trying to finish other projects and work full-time, I was not giving either thing my laser-focused attention. I had to decide what I would be an expert in before I started adding more things to my plate.

Juggling employment and self-employment can make moving up the career ladder a little slower. When people say you have to work hard to get somewhere, it is absolutely true. You may say, "Well, I've seen people move up, and they do not deserve to be where they are." They are doing something right if they have kept their position for over five years. Some of my colleagues knew what they wanted early in their careers and landed a C-suite job in their 30s, just as I did. It is definitely your choice, but if you are a young careerist, pick a lane first, perfect it, and then move on to conquer more. Always stay focused on your opportunities, not everyone else's. We all have different journeys that take us to different places.

Internships/Fellowships

For young professionals who do not have experience in the workplace, getting an internship or a fellowship to help you get your feet wet in the field you want to enter is extremely important. I was offered two internship opportunities at the same time—both in healthcare. I did not know which one to choose at the time, so I chose the one with the most community roots because that was more important to me and was aligned with my purpose in life. I was also intrigued by the uniqueness of this health system and its non-corporate structure. The ratio between male and female executives was reversed from that of corporate America. We had a female president, and the company's board was not scared to grow at lightning speed.

It's important to ask yourself a few questions when applying for an internship or fellowship:

1. What companies offer internships where you will be immersed in the company's culture and strategic initiatives?

2. What companies have fellowship programs that will help me land a full-time job with them afterward?

3. What companies have a structured and well-rounded internship or fellowship program that believes these candidates will be their next C-suite leaders?

Leading Your First Team

One thing you want when you first lead a team is to be liked and respected. I was extremely excited but also very nervous when this happened to me. I was tasked with managing a team that had been created to educate our ambulatory sites on how a clinic functions from A to Z, with a heavy concentration on revenue cycle processes. The team members were all experts in their fields who had been pulled from their departments to help this emerging department, which had no streamlined processes, benchmarks, or goals to attain. *What did they think about me? Was I too young to lead them? Did one of them think they should be leading their team instead of me? How could I help them if they knew more about the day-to-day processes than I did?* A big mistake I see other young leaders make is forcing things on people instead of getting to know them first and understanding what motivates people to do their jobs.

I felt the pressure to find a balance between addressing opportunities for improvement without coming off too strongly and unintentionally hurting someone's feelings. In a relationship, if you want to impress them, you may go out of your way and get them presents. On their birthday, you want to do something special. When you celebrate a year together, you go out and celebrate. That was what I did with my first team. I realized that I did not need to do all this to build a strong and loyal team. All they wanted was to feel respected, appreciated, cared for, and empowered to grow and bring new ideas to the table.

You will make the greatest mistakes and not understand how to handle situations with confidence until you reflect on your actions and improve your approach. The one thing I have kept ingrained in my memory from one of my mentors is, "Problems don't go away; they only get worse if you do not address them." Your first team may make you feel you aren't fit to manage people until you realize your way is not always the right way, and there is more than one way to get to point B if you allow your team to have some autonomy. That way, you will not be so frustrated when things do not go exactly as you had planned.

Perseverance

If a title means more to you than the success of the organization you work for, you may get the title, but it will not last long. I say this because I've seen people come and go, lasting in the organization for one to two years, with the same superiority complex. They will set up a meeting with you to find out what is going on with your department, but it's more like a chance for them to tell you all about their experience. I've had staff move to another organization because of a title change or because of a raise. They wanted to come back after they realized it would come with a lot more work than was disclosed at the beginning.

I'm a big proponent of looking at other options if you have exhausted your opportunities for growth in your current organization; perhaps you have talked to your boss about opportunities for growth, you have asked for projects to gain more experience and build relationships with other departments, you have mastered your position, and there are no open positions to apply for that could help you on your career journey.

I was looking into other job opportunities to leave my current position where I felt stuck. I talked to my boss, but she did not have the time to teach me any ideas she had. It seemed like she had fires to put out almost every day, so I stopped bothering her. I asked her if I could ask her boss for any projects, and she politely agreed. I ended up using one of those projects and turning it into a whitepaper I presented at the University of Jaipur in India. There are opportunities everywhere if you have the right mindset to turn a negative into something uniquely beautiful and out of your comfort zone.

Consistency

Think of your career as if you were an athlete. To be successful, you have to consistently train to improve your skills and maintain your spot as a top performer. If you haven't already begun noticing who is a top performer in your workplace or your personal life, I challenge you to do so. This will give you real-life scenarios to analyze how successful people are in maintaining their success and how much work they are still putting into their craft. You will also have the chance to ask these people what they did to get to where they are. I can assure you everyone has a different story that motivated them to keep going and breaking the mold in whatever craft they decided on.

The saying "practice makes perfect" is a term I constantly think of when I want to give up on something. I understand that if I really want something, I will have to put in the work to get there. This is a common mistake I see others miss when they are complaining about their career growth. They want everyone else to solve their problems instead of focusing on being the best they can be for their superiors to see. I attribute my success to moving up quickly by being consistently reliable. I wanted to learn to be an expert in my field and contribute to the success of any organization I worked for.

Now, fast track five, six, seven, eight, nine, or ten years in my former job as Chief Ambulatory Officer. I still wanted to learn to make our department better, but I was now in a position to help others build their confidence, get them out of their comfort zone, and grow. That's something that I love and that I can do in my current position. The molding of your career journey is in your hands. You have the power and so many resources to do what makes you happy.

CHAPTER 2

Focus on Your Purpose in Life

Finding My Purpose Early On

In high school, I went to a magnet school where they concentrated on science. I said, "Maybe I want to be a doctor, and that's how I can help people." When I went to college, I was pre-med, and I learned biology and chemistry were not for me. Having to study this material for the next ten or more years was not very appealing to my social life. Also, fainting at the sight of my own blood made me realize this would probably be an issue.

One day, I was talking to one of my colleagues who introduced me to healthcare administration. At that time, I said, "Well, why not? I definitely don't want to be pre-med, so let me try this route and still try to make a difference." Through my master's program, I realized my passion for leadership aligned with my purpose in life.

I still believed that my career goal was to get a degree, move up the ladder, and become part of the C-suite team. I did not realize until I started moving up how much more it took to get to the C-suite than I'd been taught in school. We sometimes think that having a title is the goal, but I now know that while having a title has its perks, which align with my purpose in life, it's not how I achieve success and happiness.

Finding Your Purpose

As I mentioned, my purpose in life is to help others. You may think that's an extremely broad purpose, which is intentional since I love to work on many different projects all at once. I get excited about something, then get distracted with something else, go back to the first thing I was excited about, and then say yes to five other things.

My head tends to work that way in the workplace and my personal life, so I'm always busy and sometimes don't take a breath, but I enjoy it. So when I'm in a funk and think I can't do it, I think, *Yeah, you can because your purpose is to help others.*

Maybe your purpose is to make the world a better place by choosing a plant-based lifestyle, and you want to influence others through your experiences of what to eat, what not to eat, and how that affects the environment. Or it could be coming up with the next artificial intelligence technology or an app to make life more efficient or to live a faith-based life where all your decisions revolve around your faith. Your purpose may be more specific, like being a great mother, or you may not truly know yet what your purpose in life is.

So, how do you find your purpose? A great question to ask yourself when trying to figure out what your purpose in life is: *Who am I?* When

I am trying to figure out my purpose in life, I always ask myself these questions:

1. What brings me joy?

2. How do I want to be remembered?

3. Who do I want to make the biggest impact on? Is it the world? Is it my family? Is it my child? Is it my parents?

Whatever it may be, find your purpose, so you have something to guide your life.

I always knew I wanted to find a profession where I could help the most people. Early on in elementary school, I was very protective of others. Injustice is a big trigger for me and makes me want to protect others who can't speak up for themselves. Sometimes, I've judged someone in a negative light when, in reality, it was a miscommunication between my team and that person.

So, when I first started leading my first team after starting in the ambulatory operations department, I believed everything my team said without checking. This got me into conflicts that would have been avoided if I had asked questions instead of just listening to one side of the story. Knowing when to verify what your team tells you is based on facts instead of their perception of reality is key to creating meaningful solutions. This is something that I learned and now take into consideration when making decisions or assumptions about people.

You will have influences in your life, be it your parents, significant others, or colleagues. In the end, only you know what makes you happy, not what makes others happy for you. My purpose has always been the same: to help others. But in what capacity and how much is constantly changing? I'm okay with just making a difference in one person's life but striving to help others like I have been helped throughout my career and life.

With that being said, you've got to have the right mindset to help others. It does not have as much of a positive impact if others see you are struggling to support them. The big thing is don't engage in battles that have nothing to do with you.

Rediscovering Your Purpose... When You Have To

We were at an executive strategy meeting when one of my colleagues pulled me aside after noticing my demeanor throughout the meeting. I'd started thinking about all the negative things going on around me, and I couldn't get out of that mindset. She asked me what was wrong, and I pretty much broke down. I expressed my dissatisfaction with feeling unheard and undervalued by my superiors.

As a young leader, you will tend to over-analyze and doubt yourself, but often, it's all in your head. This happened to me midway through my C-suite journey and was a deciding factor in my looking for an executive coach. This changed my entire mindset. My executive coach gave me the tools to change my perspective and reflect on situations in a constructive way. She helped me make decisions that aligned with my core values, and it took me a year to refocus on my purpose.

My executive coach showed me I could answer my own questions. I have always had a great support system filled with people who hold me accountable because they want to see me achieve my dreams, and I think that plays a big part in finding success. Whether it be your family, friends, or co-workers, surround yourself with like-minded people. If you see the world as a beautiful place, you will find your motivation and start intentionally living for your purpose. I love what I do, and I love being around people who want to make this world a better place. I surround myself with those that support me, and I support them.

My friend was the CEO of a company in Florida. She realized the role wasn't for her as she was away from her family and had to deal with disrespectful men trying to bring her down. She came to visit me while looking at a job site she was consulting at nearby, so we went to dinner. She's a Millennial minority like me. She is now enjoying her new job, where she's not in the C-suite and doesn't supervise anyone, which has made her happier with her life. She has ventured into flipping homes as well and is still in healthcare as a consultant, but she doesn't have that C-suite title, and she doesn't need it for her happiness.

If you do end up getting to the C-Suite, that doesn't mean it is for you. It wasn't for my friend, and it was a big eye-opener for me. It's not for everyone, and that's okay. At school, it was instilled in us that we should be in the C-suite, but that doesn't mean you have to do that for the rest of your life.

Stay Focused on Your Purpose

So, if you really think about it, some of these internal battles are not our own to fight. We just get so worked up because someone else is on their phone longer than they are working. They take a longer lunch than they should. They don't work as hard as you. They may always gossip about other people. Ask yourself if these are really the battles you should waste your time on and if they have nothing to do with your purpose in life. Absolutely not.

So why is focusing on your purpose in life more important than focusing on your career? Your purpose is what inherently drives you to do anything you set your mind to. I believe a career is what you study for to make a living, and with that living, you can invest in doing what makes you happy. A career can change. Your purpose is your purpose. When people get too focused on moving up the corporate ladder, they can lose sight of why they wanted the role in the first place. Being a leader means you prioritize people. It's not for a title or a pay raise—it's making a difference for others.

If you have time to think about everyone else's problems, then I would venture to say that you aren't busy enough working on yourself. Staying busy with productive tasks that yield success in your life is key. The busier you are, the less time you have to focus on negative "what ifs." Don't be afraid to ask for additional projects to figure out what your strengths are and what areas you need to improve on.

If you do not advocate for yourself, no one else is going to do that for you. My mom, my aunt, and my grandma all told me that at a very early age. Instead of questioning why my boss didn't give me this or why my boss doesn't include me in that, ask your boss to assign you a project. Trust me, if they're smart, they're going to give you work that they need to finish.

If they can't help right now, move on. Sometimes we get so stuck in ideas that she or he should do this for me. Sometimes, you may be in a position where you have grown as much as you can, or you're not learning in the capacity that you want to learn, so it's okay to pivot and try something new. It's scary, but sometimes, it's something you have to do to keep moving toward your purpose.

Surround Yourself With Like-Minded People

I've learned that when you surround yourself with individuals who share the same passion as you, you can create beautiful things together. The world is a beautiful place, and I love to be around people who are passionate about making it a better place for future generations. I've also learned that purpose-focused people inspire me to keep pushing forward with whatever new idea I have in my head.

One of my colleagues is purpose-focused, and now I am blessed to call her my best friend. We met in India when we were both presenting our papers on healthcare-related topics to a university. We were able to talk as we moved from city to city, bus ride to bus ride, connecting on a deep, intellectual level. Previously, she was a dentist in Peru, and her purpose in life was to be a successful Latina entrepreneur. She figured out the right steps, took them to find financial freedom, and is now doing what truly makes her happy. She got married, had a little girl, and is now in the investment field. She completely changed her career, but she's doing things that fit her happiness and her purpose in life.

Another purpose-focused person is one of my mentors. He went to pharmacy school but was called to develop an underserved community instead. Now, he is the owner and board member of a local bank and the hospital where I currently work. His purpose is to improve the quality of services available in our area. He is an innovator who sees opportunities and has been blessed with the ability to change the lives of many in the community. Although he had a complete career change, he never lost sight of his purpose.

Purpose-focused people are influential because their calling extends beyond their careers. I truly believe that when you have a purpose in life, you will always be driven to nurture it. Living out your purpose opens up endless possibilities for what you can achieve in your career.

I started my career journey as a pre-med student, but now I'm working in healthcare administration. Maybe in five years, I'll want to be married and stay at home. And I will achieve my purpose to help others by being a great mom and helping my children. Or maybe in ten years, I'll be running the largest health system in the world to help a community. You never know where life might take you career-wise, but your purpose will always stay the same.

CHAPTER 3

Leading Multigenerational Teams

I call myself a collector of personalities. I think humans are interesting because everyone has a different view of life. There are some individuals who say I am a Millennial, but I don't want to be perceived that way. Some individuals boast every minute that their generation was the best because of [X, Y, and Z]. Everyone is different, whether they be a Gen Z and relate more to Gen Xers or a Baby Boomer going through a midlife crisis that wants to fit into current societal trends. To obtain a baseline on generational ideals, it is understandable to group people together who were raised in the same era, but it is not okay to put everyone in that generation and say they're all the same. We're all different, and that's what makes humans beautiful.

Being an informal leader was much easier for me since I was like the cool aunt who was always the good guy, giving my opinion from the sidelines. When I was a special projects coordinator, I spoke to different leaders and offered them advice when they came to me, venting about what they should do with their employees.

When I stepped into a leadership position, I was now in a different department. It was a department that needed a lot of tender loving care; it had grown too fast, and there were really no processes in place. The goal of this department would be to use their expertise to train others. When I first met them, I acknowledged their expertise in their field and made it my mission to become an expert, too. I knew that I could lead this team to reach its full potential, but I needed to take steps to see how we could work together. Leading teams with multiple generations is a big hot topic in the workforce.

Multi-Generational Communication

Having four generations in the workforce is awesome but also challenging. You not only get to see how people think differently but also get to experience various communication styles. Some would rather text, and some like emails, whereas a Millennial like me would rather text and email with the occasional phone call.

Many from Generation X would rather meet face-to-face or get on a phone call. I split my time as a leader. First, I have face-to-face meetings with clinic directors to discuss action items that I need to assist with. Then, I have face-to-face team meetings with clinic managers where we communicate information that everyone needs to know. Text messages are used for short questions to which my team needs an immediate answer instead of waiting for when we meet face-to-face.

Phone calls are for different generations. Instead of a long text where it gets miscommunicated, I've learned just to pick up the phone and ask for what is truly needed, as text messages read in haste can be misunderstood. Communication is very important to me, and I communicate effectively by utilizing emails, newsletters, text messages, repeating things, having face-to-face meetings, and doing Zoom calls. By doing this, we can reach every generation's communication style.

Because of my position now, I oversee around 1200 employees in my department (20 percent of the company's workforce), making it a little more challenging for me to get to know everyone personally. Our newsletter is also really important for highlighting new changes and is another platform to share information. We recently implemented fireside chats with frontline staff to gain perspective on day-to-day operations. During these chats, I ask about their career goals, personal goals, and why they chose to be a part of our organization.

Delivering Multi-Generational Praise

Understanding how people feel appreciated is a big part of being a leader. Nowadays, the economy is not as great as we would like, and monetary recognition is valued differently. Some generations have the mentality that if they go above and beyond, they just want their leader to recognize the work that they do. Sometimes, baking or bringing something you made from home shows that you care. A personalized letter shows that you spent time expressing your appreciation on paper.

Last year, we developed a get-to-know-me questionnaire. We had everyone fill it out to eliminate guessing. Everything was in the form, from their favorite birthday cake to their preferred communication style and even pet peeves. Now, when we have a new employee join our department, we know what they like and what they don't like, so we can personalize our recognition of them as individuals.

Generational Motivational Drive

From what I have seen, motivation to work is different across generations. Some generations feel that they should come to work and just work. Some feel they should come to work and have a family dynamic and fun. I truly believe that has changed over the years. People are now choosing to work where they are in an environment that feels like family and where they can be creative and happy. In the past ten years, work culture has shifted to become a culture of support, respect, happiness, creativity, and innovation.

Those from Gen X and the older generations will probably stay in their current positions because they're closer to retirement age and don't want to job-hop. They just want to have the respect that they deserve. These individuals will likely stay with an organization for a long time, so find ways to make their experience more enjoyable.

Some Millennials and Gen Zs are currently in their first job. Their way of thinking and their motivations are different since this is probably not the job they'll be in forever or will retire from. As leaders, we should be thinking about jobs for them that are at a higher level that they can grow into and how we can help them get there. There may be even younger employees for whom this is just a job so they can finish their degree. Ask those employees about their degree plan and see if it aligns with their current role so that when they graduate, there's something already in the organization that you can help them transition into. It's important to invest in people because it builds loyalty towards one another. You care about me, and I care about you. If you care about the organization and your department being the best, then I will help you do that because you're investing in me.

I recently attended a meeting with all executives where we were asked who was thinking outside the box. There was a show of hands; the ones who raised their hands were all Millennials. After discussing this with my peers, I realized that Millennial leaders are the ones who are still trying to find out how to improve not only themselves but also all departments. At the same time, you have other executives who just want to do what they're paid to do. And as Millennials, we're still not at the level where we think we will end up, and we want to grow. And in that sense, we're helping the organization. After this discussion, I truly understood the importance of having such a diverse team, even in the C-suite, because everyone's motivation to work is different. And once you understand that, it helps you build a better and stronger team, a united one.

Leading a Highly Skilled Team

It is important to give a highly skilled team meaningful work. Give them projects where they are willing to innovate and put in the extra hours. I oversee a business intelligence department where I trust that they are the experts who can abstract and present data in a way that others can easily understand. I let the team know what I need but give them the freedom to make it make sense. It's their work that they're proud of because they developed it with my vision in mind. So, when leading a highly skilled team, it's great to brainstorm. Ask them to be part of the decision-making process because their thought process can develop ideas that you probably never even thought of because that is not the way you think. This will alleviate micromanaging since they are a part of creating the process from the beginning. From there, things are easier, fewer questions are asked, there are fewer tweaks, and more growth.

Highly skilled individuals could be the best potential mentors for new employees coming in. Ask them if they want an intern, if that's possible in the organization, or maybe they want to present something for the entire team to get help on. Give this group the opportunity to share their skills and knowledge with others. In my experience, they usually find it very rewarding.

Collaborative Leadership

Including others in your decision-making process is key to your success. As a first-time leader, I tried to make decisions for everyone, but then I didn't think about this, and I didn't think about that, and I didn't think that this process would affect that process. So, after a few mistakes, I learned I needed to involve as many people as possible to avoid recurring errors.

Collaborative leadership is extremely important; the more ideas you have, the better the outcome. Sometimes, you think, *Well, I don't have the time to meet with my team,* but they are there to help you. So meeting with your team should be your priority. It could be a five-minute huddle. It could be a weekly meeting where you touch base for 15 minutes. It could be a monthly meeting in a bigger group setting where you've invited different departments to share the changes that potentially affect your department. You could have a one-on-one where it's just you and the direct report that you need to share information with sooner rather than later. Having all the facts from other subject matter experts will always be the best way to make decisions.

Focus on Individuals, Not Generational Stigmas

Take a chance on people, see what they show, and from there, decide based on real actions, not because of a generational stigma.

There are six things that have helped me lead all generations equally:

1. Be empathetic to situations that are out of your control. If someone is consistently running late because there's a personal issue at home, we sometimes make a quick judgment that they're not good employees because of an issue that we are unaware of or haven't thought about. I believe everyone who comes to work wants to do the very best they can.

It is not realistic to think that people can keep their personal problems at home. The way they feel at home will spill into the workplace because we're not robots; those are our feelings, and we can't turn our emotions on and off. So, once you know that someone is going through something, instead of trying to punish their short-term behavior, you need to be more empathetic and learn to adapt when things happen. Think about how you would like to be treated if you were in that same situation.

2. Trust your team to do their job. If you don't currently trust your team, what steps are you taking to build trust in them? Having a frank conversation with people will get you further than assuming that they can't do their job. A lack of communication can lead to making assumptions. It could be a report that wasn't completed, but your direct report didn't even have access to the file, so they couldn't complete the task.

If you're a leader and your direct reports are managers, and their direct reports are supervisors, and the supervisor's direct reports are front-line staff, you should not be micromanaging every little task. You may need to ask yourself if you're ready to be a leader and figure out how to give up control.

3. Deal with uncomfortable situations before they worsen. Problems don't go away. They need to be dealt with even if they're uncomfortable or you really like an employee and don't understand why they are acting out; you can always find a solution. If you don't address it, things tend to worsen because that employee does not know they're doing something wrong or may need additional help.

There are going to be times when there are employees who aren't the best cultural fit and do more damage to the overall team dynamic. They may be the best employees, but not the best teammates. And if you let it snowball, you'll tend to lose the team you don't want to lose because you have not addressed the issue at hand with that individual.

4. Learn to adapt to every personality. Once you learn to adapt to people's personalities, you are not thinking that everyone should be like you. Honestly, having a hundred or a thousand Veronicas would be a very boring life. I would not enjoy that at all. Everyone is completely different as to how they navigate their lives. You would want some leniency when something goes wrong, and others deserve the same.

People react differently to situations. I may feel very passionate about a topic that someone else doesn't think is a big deal, and that is okay. When I hear one of my directors or managers vent about a certain situation, I understand that they're passionate about their point of view, but they need to understand that others may not feel the same.

5. Don't judge a book by its cover. There was a young woman who wanted to join the team. She came to talk to me before she applied to one of my staff positions and asked if I could take a chance on her. I thought it took a lot of courage to come up to me, knowing that she didn't have the experience that others may have had, and I appreciated her hunger. I realized she would need to be coached and mentored by the team to get to where she wanted to be, but I realized she had something to prove, and she wasn't going to stop until she achieved her goal.

Early on, she was very much judged by her appearance as she looked like a Mexican Barbie who knew how to dress, and she carried herself in a confident and classy demeanor. I knew this perception would cause some unintentional jealousy because she was not only beautiful on the outside but even more beautiful on the inside. She broke all barriers in her role and built relationships due to her professionalism, willing-to-serve attitude, and work ethic. When she finally moved to another company for career growth, I was extremely proud. I didn't have a spot for her at that moment for her career growth, but I still keep in touch with her as I'm hopeful we will cross paths again.

Thankfully, I have seen fewer judgments from leaders about employees' tattoos, piercings, rainbow-colored hair, and many other physical appearance details that honestly have no bearing on anyone's work ethic. Instead of judging, appreciate people who are comfortable in their own skin and express their individuality.

6. Let go of people who are not a good cultural fit. When you see potential in someone and want to give them a chance, you might put them in a role where they completely surprise you and not in a good way. There has to be a point where even if you care about this person as an individual, you wonder how much you can take or how fair it is to the organization that they are not doing the job expected of them. So those tough decisions have to be addressed before they turn into a snowball effect, and you start losing people because of this individual.

Instead of cutting ties with one person, you're now cutting ties with five people because you kept that person in a role that they just weren't fit for. I actually had an experience with an individual where we worked together side by side. We had the same boss, and then I took his role, and she reported to me. She did a great job; she was super smart and an expert in her field, but she really didn't know how to manage her team. Half of her team had resigned, and a month later, she resigned by email and walked out. I asked HR to investigate what was going on because such a trend suggests a common denominator. I wondered if I had blinders on because I'd thought she was great. I clearly didn't know everything that had been going on. I didn't realize she was belittling her staff and literally making them break down to a point where they had to seek counseling. *Could I have coached her? Being a new leader, could I have saved the team? Could I have put communication channels in place so her team felt they could come to me earlier?*

One of her team members told me why she was leaving, saying she wanted more of a work-life balance and wasn't feeling herself. I oversee a counseling clinic, so I called to make her an appointment to get her help. She's actually back in the organization, and she always thanks me. I didn't understand why she was thanking me until I asked her. She explained that it was because I helped her get the support she needed, and she now felt comfortable enough to share why she needed it. She told me it was due to constant belittling from the previous team leader. This surprised me because I didn't realize how deep-rooted the issue was, and it taught me to examine if there's a trend of turnover.

If someone's showing you who they are, believe them.

CHAPTER 4

Always Be Yourself

Some people will love you. Some people will dislike you. Most people will just go along with their day and really not think about you at all. Ask yourself:

1. Do I want to make an extra effort to not be myself?

2. Do I want to go with the flow because I want to be liked?

3. Do I want to be the person who always says, "I wish I had said that?"

I was at lunch with a few colleagues discussing work relationships, and one story really stuck with me. One of my colleagues had a friend, and eventually, they ended up working together. He quickly noticed her personality and demeanor were different at work. He thought she was an amazing person who always put others first. But in work life, he started to see that she was a completely different person. She would belittle people, gossip about them, and create lies to make others look bad. He realized that she felt so insecure in her role that she needed to put others down to stay relevant. At lunch that day, I asked my friend how that made him feel. He said, "I really feel sad for her."

I took a step back and said, "I can't blame her because she's been living in survival mode for a long time, constantly trying to prove that she belongs."

I always tell people, "Be yourself." Once you're not, you start regretting things, resenting people, and acting out because you begin to lose your identity.

Many people want to please their team. It's okay if others have an opinion about you or don't see eye to eye with your decision. We don't want to not do what's right because we're too focused on people's feelings. As a leader, the decisions I make will not always be well-received by every single person. It's okay that people vent about you, but it's how you deal with it that can make or break you. You can either sulk and not move forward or realize it's part of life and carry on.

I've always known I needed to take care of those who weren't as confident to speak up for themselves. Has that gotten me in trouble throughout my career? Yes, because people started relying on me to defend them in every situation. Now, instead of taking on everyone's problems, I ask them, "What are you doing about it? Do you want to stay like that? Do you want to feel like that? Who have you escalated it to?" By asking these questions, I encourage others to get out of their comfort zone and learn to self-advocate.

Deciding Your Next Move

Staying true to yourself is extremely important when you're making decisions, especially about your career growth. For example, you wouldn't want to remain in a position where there are no growth opportunities. If you've told your boss you want to move up, and they've asked you, "Well, what do you want to do?" but there are no open positions further up the ladder, what do you say? Do you stay there or stay true to yourself and say, "I'm going to get out of my comfort zone and move on?"

I was in a position like this, housed in the broom closet, according to my former boss. I was so bored that I would create initiatives to improve our department because I had run out of work to do. At this point, I realized I needed to either leave this organization or figure out where else I could grow. Thankfully, my former boss had just started in the department that I currently oversee and took me under his wing. This kick-started my journey to growth and learning at the same organization.

He moved at a quick pace and did not care to piss off the wrong people to do the right thing. His agenda was to better the department at lightning speed, which rocked the boat since no one was used to this innovative and collaborative leadership style. We had overcommunication with meetings and trackers that had every item each of his direct reports had to follow up on. He was very process-focused, but we also knew that he had our backs if we ever needed help in pushing our projects along. Not everyone worked at his speed, and not everyone was in their role for the right reasons; some were more self-serving. Thankfully, those individuals were weeded out over the years. One of my mentors always says, "Your boss laid the foundation that helped you create the culture this department has needed for a long time."

Tweaking Your Leadership Style

When leading a team, I always say, "Work is work." However figuring out the best way to lead a team where there is motivation, creativity, and respect for one another is the challenging part. Staying true to yourself as a leader but knowing that there are different ways to lead a team is something that you have to keep in mind.

When I am asked what leaders give me guidance, I usually respond that I learn from all leaders, from excellent to not-so-excellent leaders, but mostly the not-so-excellent leaders. From them, I learn what *not* to do.

Think about a time when your friends or colleagues were venting to you about their superior. You most likely remember the negative parts of the story, and these are the kinds of things you can learn from that you should not take into your leadership style as you now know how this affects someone negatively.

When it comes to excellent leaders, I ask myself: *Do they lift other people up because they are proud to see people succeed? Do they place the needs of others before their own when making decisions? Do they understand the needs of their employees?* It's really important to observe and learn from other people's leadership styles so you don't have to start from scratch. You can pick and choose what traits you want to take from them.

Identifying Your Strengths and Core Values

I've always tried to be the best leader I can be, but there was a time when I was in a funk, so I invested in an executive coach. She opened my world to limitless possibilities if I wanted to pursue them. We started off with assessments (needs, values, and strength assessments like Gallup's CliftonStrengths assessment), and at first, I didn't understand why I was taking them. I thought I would tell her my issues, and then she would coach me about how to solve them. However, I didn't realize that I would be solving my own problems by channeling into my inner mentor.

The assessments and her guidance led to a complete transformation after we learned my core values. With those assessments, she was able to pick the best methods for coaching me. There are many assessments out there on the internet to see what your strengths are. What do I need to work on? What are my values? And are those values really aligned with the culture and vision of the organization where I work?

My executive coach helped me identify my values and needs, learn how to make decisions based on my values, and get out of my funk by evaluating whether my work and personal environment were meeting and fulfilling my needs.

My top six values are:

1. **Learning.** I'm a lifelong learner. I love to pick up new things, and I am passionate about knowing the latest innovations and implementing them in my daily life.

2. **Being a Catalyst.** This means I want to make an impact on the world. I want to move things to create an impact.

3. **Teaching.** The third one for me is teaching. I love to educate. I want people to grow, and the only way for them to grow is to teach. I love to share my knowledge and do something that others can benefit from.

4. **Contribution and Service.** My fourth strength is contribution and service. I like to assist others to help them grow, which aligns with my servant leadership style.

5. **Leadership.** My fifth one is leadership and influencing others by being the best that I can be to help others. This aligns with my purpose and reminds me to keep perfecting my leadership skills.

6. **Creativity.** Thankfully, I'm in a career field that is ever-changing. Being able to continuously create has confirmed my love for healthcare as it fits in with my values and strengths.

Your needs will change with the different milestones in your life, but your values will always stay the same. At this time, my top five needs are freedom, integrity, honesty, accomplishment, and peace. But your needs will change, and that's okay. Knowing your needs brings you a perspective and opens up your eyes so you can ask yourself, *Am I fulfilling my needs? Or why am I so burned out? Is it because my needs aren't being met?* It gives you that cheat sheet to help you find more work-life balance.

Channel Your Inner Mentor

When you're staying true to yourself and understanding your values and needs, you're constantly talking to yourself, and you know yourself better than anyone else. Your mom may think they know you the best, or maybe your spouse, your dad, or your grandparents, but the person who knows you the best is yourself. You don't share all your feelings and emotions and what you're thinking in your head with one specific person every day, all the time. They're not in the shower with you while you're having a conversation in your mind, trying to see what you need to do. The most important decisions that I have made have been by talking to myself. I didn't realize this successful exercise until my executive coach pointed it out, and it really made me take a step back and think about how I make decisions. I have my own ways of making decisions, and it is important to remember that your process is your own. The beauty of being human is that we are all different, which means we all have a unique perspective. We all see beauty through our own eyes. For example, architecture and art have many styles based on who created the idea and brought it to life.

Your Upbringing Molds You

I believe your upbringing defines your personality and the way you navigate your life. Society has labeled generations to differentiate their culture. We listened to the same music, and we had access to the same technology and media outlets to feed us information. This most likely differs from past and future generations.

Think about what you cherish the most in life or what experiences you will always remember that helped make you the person you are today. If I were to guess, most of these moments were complex situations where you overcame something by putting in extra effort to change something you decided you were not going to tolerate anymore. So, from there, you start building your personality and figuring out your definition of happiness. I truly believe making mistakes is the best way to learn and correct moving forward so that you don't have to make them again. If you overthink everything, you will never complete anything because you are striving for perfection. I would never want to be perfect. I think that would be boring. I wouldn't even know what perfection would look like because that is different for everyone. I feel if you navigate your life by mimicking someone else's, you will never be fulfilled.

I can only give guidance on my own experiences, those of my peers, and those of my friends. But I still stress that your best mentor is yourself. When making a big decision, stop asking others what they think is the best for you. When thinking about your happiness, take a step back and think of the times you laughed the hardest, had the most fun, and loved the deepest. Use those memories to guide you on your path to becoming the best version of yourself.

Finding a Career That Fits You

When thinking about your next career move, think about how much you're willing to sacrifice to learn the role. Do you have the time right now to give something up? Or is this something that you would think about in a year because you will get married, start a family, or need a break to fulfill your energy? When making big life changes, talk to yourself because, at the end of the day, you know what you need to do. You know what decision you need to make to make yourself happy.

Forge your own path to success. Get out of your comfort zone. Young leaders often avoid this, maybe because they're timid or embarrassed about making mistakes or failing. When I first started working, I would get nervous, my throat would make some sort of sound, my voice would crack, I didn't know where to look, and then I had to go back to a PowerPoint slide and read it word for word. I knew that public speaking was something that I needed to do more of to get better, but how was I going to perfect that? How was I going to practice? I asked my leader at the time if I could present anything and everything she would allow me to do.

I took every opportunity to create PowerPoints and present them to others. This was something that was out of my comfort zone, but at least I knew the directors that I was speaking to. That helped me get comfortable, know how much I needed to practice, how I was going to engage the crowd, if I was going to add stories or read off the slides, and if people would be receptive to the information I was giving them. To this day, this has helped me tremendously because if I didn't have that practice, I wouldn't be able to speak to over 200 physicians every quarter or to board members of the organization that I work at. I am now speaking at different conferences and doing podcasts and virtual webinars. I would not have gotten out of my comfort zone if I had not had this practice. If I look back, I'm not sure what setbacks I may have experienced or if it would have taken me longer to get to where I am now.

Am I perfect at public speaking? Absolutely not. Do I still get nervous? Absolutely. Do I still prepare and figure out what flow I'm going to present to the audience to see what I want them to take from my presentation? Absolutely. I'm a lifelong learner. I accept that my public speaking skills are something that I will continuously need to try to improve due to the fact that I'm not an extroverted person. So, knowing who I am and what I need to prepare has helped me know I can't just pick up the mic and start babbling about what's going on. I have to be prepared by anticipating what questions I will get asked so I have all my facts straight. If you're like me and don't like speaking, practice.

Sometimes, we feel embarrassed about doing this or that, but everyone gets embarrassed. Just learn to laugh at yourself. Life doesn't have to be that serious. I started being more confident, knowing that things were going to go wrong, and getting comfortable with that. I'm a very clumsy person, and gravity isn't my friend. So early on, I knew how to laugh at myself because I knew others were going to, and it was funny. At the end of the day, you get embarrassed because you want to get embarrassed. Identify what will and won't get you to the next level, and be prepared to chase it.

Finding Your Happiness

Your happiness is *your* happiness. We all define happiness differently. I'm at a place right now where my happiness is not going after the next best thing in my career but appreciating what we have built as a team and finding ways to make things better with a more relaxed approach. I truly trust my team. We're all very honest. I have an open-door policy. I have built a relationship with them so they know they won't get in trouble for doing something wrong. They can make mistakes, and it's okay. I have their back.

My happiness last year was found in speaking at conferences about our operational and financial initiatives. My happiness during the pandemic in 2020 was to work every day and figure out how we were going to keep everyone safe at work and not break down. My happiness when I was an intern was to try to learn as much as I could so I could apply it to what I was learning in school.

Obviously, to know what happiness is, you have to understand sadness. Work-life is definitely not all rainbows and roses. Some people only want what's best for themselves. Some people have never been called out for their inappropriate behavior. When you stay true to yourself and know what your happiness is, you tend to deal with things that are not rainbows and roses differently. You don't react, or you don't stay quiet. You stay true to who you are and understand what you're going to tolerate and how to set those barriers and expectations for others to treat you the way you want to be treated.

Addressing Your Barriers

I've heard countless stories from friends, women, and men where there have been extremely inappropriate power plays. At the time that it was happening, they really didn't know how to react to the behavior. I had a friend in my year who was following the same path I was. She was extremely excited about her internship. We checked up on each other for six months, and one day, she came to me and said, "Bro, I don't really know how to handle this situation. I don't work with this individual, but he's in the C-suite, and he left a Post-it note on my desktop when I was at lunch that said, *'Are you wearing panties?'*" It was extremely shocking because she completely respected this individual. She thought he was assisting her in her growth, and when she was stuck, she would ask him for help. She never thought that this would lead to an inappropriate comment being left on her desktop. She wondered if she'd said anything that may have made him think it was okay to leave this on her desktop. Did she laugh too much with him or spend too much time in his office?

She started blaming herself instead of just taking a step back. We talked about it, and I said, "I understand that you probably don't want to hurt his feelings, and you have a good working relationship with him. It may have been a joke, but I would return the Post-it and have a conversation with him about it. Say something like, 'This is probably not something that you thought was inappropriate, or maybe you thought it was a joke, but I'm going to hand it back to you because I don't want you to get in trouble if someone else saw it.'" That was my advice to her at the time, and they still have a great working relationship, and that boundary has never been crossed again. This was the best possible scenario for her, but there are other times when the individual might start gaslighting you, and you need to explore more direct solutions.

So, things will happen, but my best advice for inappropriate power plays is to take a step back and think, *How am I going to address this?* Behaviors like that will continue if they haven't been addressed. And these are hard truths that most people don't write about or talk about because they're too embarrassed.

I recently went on a trip with some girlfriends, and we were talking about how we don't talk about inappropriate power plays, especially when you're a young leader trying to move up, and you don't want to get on anyone's bad side. We were sharing stories, and a friend told us she had hosted a provider dinner for a customer who wanted her to feed him. We were quiet and shocked that our kindhearted friend had experienced that. When we asked her what she did, she said, "I froze, but thankfully, another provider at that dinner saw how uncomfortable I was and said, 'Hey, I have a question about the drug; can we talk about it?'" And that was how she got out of it.

There's not really the right way to handle inappropriate power plays, especially when women or men feel they can't do anything about it because of the situation they're in or don't want to do anything about it because they don't think it will happen again. We are the only ones who have control over what we allow and what boundaries we set with people. Stay true to yourself as much as you can, talk yourself through making decisions, know what your values are, and know that your happiness this day, this week, and this year is really up to you.

CHAPTER 5

Say YES to Everything

I'm not sure if it's the thrill of something new or the competitiveness within myself to always do better that makes it extremely hard for me to say no to things. If I have the mental and physical ability to do whatever new task is presented to me, I usually always accept new opportunities. This thought process of having the right physical and mental mindset started a few years ago, after getting to a point where I was saying yes to everything without taking a step back, looking at my overly demanding calendar, and figuring out the amount of time an additional task would take to complete. I was so eager not to miss an opportunity that I never asked if this request could be postponed to a more ideal time that fit my schedule. I used to get agitated and frustrated because I couldn't complete the tasks I was actually responsible for in my nine-to-five job. So, I started placing myself first and asking:

1. Is this something I'm saying yes to just to please others or is this something I'm saying yes to because I'm going to learn something from this experience?

2. Do I have the time to spend on this task without feeling over-whelmed?

3. Can I move some project deadlines to fit in this new task?

4. Is this request something I can do at a later time, or is this opportunity only a one-time deal?

I ask myself those questions now when I am asked to speak at an event, coach someone, participate in committees, or even sit on a board.

Don't Only Say Yes to the Easy Things

If you are still wanting to grow in your career, you really need to focus on tasks that are challenging and completely new to you. You need to say yes to easy things to perfect the skills that you currently have, but there should be other things you prioritize too. Become an expert at them and build your confidence to remind you of your worth. Sometimes, people want to do the easy stuff so they can feel okay. Once you have that attitude, or you are in a funk, you may want to get out of it by doing something you know you can easily get done. But saying yes to only easy things will not get you to the level you may want to reach.

Trying new things is an opportunity to learn and adds valuable skills to your resume, portfolio, and when you're talking to people in meetings. You may like or dislike doing new things, but if you don't try them, you will never know. Try something that's unknown at least once, and if you don't like it, then you know you can say no the next time because it was not an experience or task that fit your needs or values. New things are not only for growth but also for experience. Once you get to know new things and experience them, you can talk about them to others.

Quality Over Quantity

There are only a certain number of hours per day, depending on how much sleep you need to function. If you have numerous projects going on, they will probably not be completed in time. The quality of work may suffer if you take on too much. It can be difficult to focus on each project because your brain is switching back and forth between five different projects. When you're working on multiple projects, you may be 60 percent finished on one, and you're working on something else that you're at 20 percent, and then you're working on another one that you're at 80 percent. Your mind is everywhere, so it's difficult to take a step back and look at the details. The quality of work may not be as great because you have too many things going on, and your work-life balance will not be ideal. Juggling all these projects was incredibly hard for me at the beginning of my career. It was hard to get organized and say yes to the right things for my career journey.

Do Things Because You Really Believe In Them, Not to Seek Any Type of Validation or Appreciation

I've learned that if you are looking for validation from people, you will always be disappointed. I used to take on every little task that someone wanted me to do because I looked up to them, and I wanted them to know I was doing a great job. I finally asked myself, *Why do I need this validation from this individual who does not know what I do every day, does not know all the struggles I have, and doesn't know that it's affecting my personal life or lack thereof?* I used to be told I was married to my job. At first, I thought that was a compliment and that people thought I was hard-working, but I didn't realize how much it was taking a toll on my personal life. I stopped going out to events and meeting new friends. It was home, work, and gym for me until I finally snapped out of it and said, *I really need to be intentional about what I'm going to say yes to.* I wanted to do the very best at my job but also do things that made me feel happy and fulfilled. I didn't want to wake up when I was older and regret not living my life for myself.

I couldn't tell you what the breaking point was for me, but it really opened up my eyes to be more intentional because I was losing myself to get validation from others when I really didn't need that to make me happy. I then started focusing on what my leadership team needed. I started focusing on spreading my knowledge to other healthcare executives at healthcare conferences, which made me happy. I stayed focused on saying yes to things that benefited the people I cared about. I stopped looking to others for validation. That's how I was able to find my work-life balance. Everyone's work-life balance is different. Mine is probably 60-40 work-personal now. It used to be 70-30. For some of my team members, it's 50-50, and that's great. It's completely different for everyone because our values and our needs are different.

Learning to Say No

So, how do you learn to say no? What if you're a young leader, you're trying to move up, you just got out of college, or maybe you're an executive still trying to learn to say no? There are times when the only answer needs to be no. When you are climbing the career ladder, make sure you know your worth when accepting a promotion. I've seen this over and over where you're in an organization, and they promote you because you're doing a great job. Instead of just saying thank you for the promotion, make sure you get what is fair. That is something that is up to us to know what we're worth. We need to communicate with people. When I was up for a promotion, I was given an increase that, to me, did not make sense. I would have to do my job plus take on all the responsibilities of this new role, and I just wanted to be compensated fairly. I took a step back. I jotted down my thoughts and concluded I couldn't take this increase because I was already working late hours and almost every weekend with what I was doing before. I declined at that time due to the dollar amount and explained my reasoning. If I hadn't spoken up for myself, then I would have resented the role and the organization. It was very hard for me to say no because I wanted the role and to be given a chance to gain that experience at such a young age, but I knew my worth, and I fought for it.

I like to know everything about a work situation to be able to share with others and to have some input into how we could fix things. One of our team members told me she wanted to be a manager. She was great at what she did, and HR said she was super excited, but she countered on what she thought her new responsibilities would be compared to her current responsibilities. Instead of wondering why she would counter when she was the one who wanted the position, I was proud of her because she knew what it would take for her to be the best manager. Make sure you know your worth when you're accepting a promotion. You know how much you're going to put into it and how much more responsibility it's going to be. Nothing in life is free, so don't settle.

I used to always say yes when someone asked me to join a committee or organization. Luckily, my assistant reminds me that I don't always have the time, and I need to be intentional with how I spend it. I used to double- or triple-book myself. Of course, I'm not a clone, and I don't have a twin or a triplet, so I could only be in one place at one time. Now I ask myself, *Do I have the time to set aside to be part of this particular committee or organization? What value is this committee going to do for me? Is this a group of individuals I want to spend time with?*

There are tons of committees and organizations out there. Find the ones that align with your values and needs and only join those. Do some research before saying yes to being part of an organization or a committee. Ask what time commitment they need so you can ask yourself, *Is this going to make me happy? Am I going to have enough time to do it?*

When you are great at what you do, people ask you to help with other projects. I've seen this over and over, where we, as leaders, tend to give more responsibility to the people that we trust and to the people that we know are going to get it done in a timely manner. Sometimes, we need to take a step back and consider how much work they currently have and if it is possible to give them another project. In the past, I have asked young leaders, "Do you have other projects that you need to complete before taking on a new task?" At the end of the day, you're responsible for your projects, and others are responsible for their projects.

There was a time when I would get asked by different departments to assist or to be part of their subcommittees, but I would ask myself, *Do I have the time to help other departments, or do I have projects that my team needs assistance with?* Whether it's onboarding a new provider, analyzing financials, expanding a service line, or adding more resources to see more patients, it is important to build a team that can provide support. As leaders, we want to build relationships with others, and we may want to say yes to everything, but we also need to focus on our team and our projects first. If my team is good and my projects are on track, then yes, I can help.

When I wasn't this good at saying no to extra projects, I was told by one of our board members to stay in my lane. At first, I didn't understand that. I didn't understand why I was getting that feedback, but then I realized people who give you feedback have had more experience than you, and it's because they've made these mistakes. So, I really took that advice because I did have a lot on my plate. I was fairly new to the department, and it needed structure. The growth in my department was extremely high, so we were trying to keep up with the demand. I still wanted to help others because that's just inherently who I am. But I now tell people, "Stay in your lane, perfect that, and then help others." I sometimes struggle, but not like I used to. There are only so many hours, and you still need to do your job to get where you want to be.

Analyzing Your Routines to Make Space for Yes Items

I'm not the most organized person. I am always thinking about ten new ideas and another ten items on my list to complete at work. I have papers all over my desk, but if someone else moves anything, I can't find it. I know what's on my desk, and I know the order of my Post-it notes and where I place them in priority on all three of my computers. Knowing that I'm not the most organized has helped.

When you organize your calendar, I suggest tracking your personal life and work responsibilities together. Why? Because your work may not be eight-to-five. You may have work events that are after hours. You may have work events on the weekends. So when you have one calendar that you can fit both personal and work items into, you know Thursday might be a long day, so perhaps you shouldn't say yes to a friend's dinner that evening—it might be best to let them know that you're available the next day. I can say yes to more things and not have to cancel or reschedule with friends, family, or my team and colleagues at work because I have everything in one, very organized calendar.

Figure out what mental health hobby you have and stick with it. I'm not a very emotional person. I internalize a lot of my emotions. Since I was 15, I've always gone to the gym and exercised. I currently have a personal trainer because I don't like thinking about what I need to do next at the gym. I prefer to be told what I need to do. From 5 a.m.

to 6 a.m. I have a great workout, and that really prepares me for my day. It gets anything internalized in my body out and has helped me to keep a more balanced lifestyle.

What routines can you automate or have someone else do for you? There are so many tasks that have to be completed each day. We have single, working moms and dads, and we also understand that people have personal lives. So, think about what you can automate, whether it be your work or something in your personal routine. For me, it's cleaning my house. I asked myself if I had three to five hours a week to clean my house or if it was more cost-effective for me to hire someone. This allowed me the freedom to spend those three hours working on personal projects or working on emails that I didn't get through last week. We need to take a look at all of our routines and ask, *Do I really need to do those, or can I delegate those to someone else?*

Reserving your Energy

Some things are out of your control. Taking care of yourself so you can be the best leader is crucial. Delegating and not holding on to everything is important because you cannot do everything on your own. You need people to help you. There's so much that you can do and so much that you can't. Choose your battles wisely. Do I really need to waste my energy trying to debunk a myth or trying to explain a topic that no one wants to or is going to understand?

I've learned how to pick my battles. Why am I going to get upset over something I have no control over and is not contributing to my values or needs? There are times when we need to ask, *What is taking all my energy? Why am I waking up exhausted? What did I do the day before that is making my energy so low that I can't be a hundred percent productive?* Sometimes, there's no need to debate, even if an issue in your department gets brought up. Taking a step back, listening, and collecting your thoughts are most important. Maybe scheduling a one-on-one conversation with your peer or executive is the way to go. Letting them know I didn't really understand what they meant and asking them to elaborate may clarify the issue that was presented.

You are the only person who knows the best way for you to spend your time on the weekends. Sometimes, it will be with your friends, reading a book, or completing a project, but only you know what will give you the energy you need. Sometimes, I want to hang out with my friends the entire weekend, but I know that come Monday, I'm going to be exhausted. On other weekends, I just want to watch a movie with my dog or read a book to reflect on other things. Know how much energy you need to reserve to be a hundred percent the next day.

Let your team be part of committees so they can be involved in what is going on. I would double- or triple-book myself because I wanted to be on every committee. I wanted to know everything that was going on, and then I would share it with my team. As I took on more responsibilities, it became increasingly difficult. So now, if I am part of a committee at the hospital, I have a representative from my department that goes to the meetings. That not only frees up my time but also gives my team more experience. This makes me happy because it gives my team the opportunity to be in the spotlight and show their strengths to other people.

Although saying yes is very important for you to get out of your comfort zone, you are the only one who knows what you should say yes to and what you should say no to right now. Will there be lost opportunities? Sure. Will there be other opportunities that are more aligned with your purpose? Absolutely. Never regret your decisions. There are so many possibilities in this world. It really is what you make of it. Time will tell.

CHAPTER 6

Success Is Not Achieved Without Support

Early on in my career, the best lessons were observing others handle situations and learning from their mistakes and wins. It is not always what people tell you but what they actually show you that you should believe. Remember, the only person you can change is yourself.

Success is not achieved without support. You will not move up to the top alone. If anyone has told you that, it is not true. You need people and their support to help you get to where you want to be. Before moving to Houston to start my master's program in business and healthcare administration, I wanted to get my feet wet in healthcare, so I started working at a private practice clinic. My friend got me the job, and I was really excited to work and learn about the specialty.

I interviewed with the physician she knew and started working in the front. I would make calls and do all types of administrative duties that they needed. At first, it was really fun, and I was always asking what else I could do. I didn't know anything about healthcare, so I tried to learn as much as I could during my time there.

One day, the manager assigned me a project for which I needed a clipboard, which I took from the front desk. The registration person got upset and asked why I was taking her clipboard. I said I needed it to work on a project, and she had four other ones. She handed me a broken clipboard. At first, I took it, but when she was with a patient, I took a functioning clipboard back to my desk. While I was walking back, I felt a tug on my ponytail. I never thought someone would pull my hair over a clipboard in a work environment, but it happened.

At this time, I had little experience working in toxic environments. I could not believe what had happened, and I completely shut down and started crying because I didn't realize that things like that could actually happen to me. I still tell people this story because we are so quick to judge on first impressions without giving people the chance to get to know the real you. When I calmed down and talked to the manager of the clinic, she said, "Well, the reason she feels like that is because the provider has told the staff that you work under him, and no one can tell you anything." I didn't realize that the provider had put a target on my back and labeled me as a favorite. The office manager calmed me down and said, "I'm pretty sure that he mentioned that, so they would be open to letting you shadow them, but maybe they thought you were going to replace them." When things like this happen, you need people to support you. There was one individual who started at the same time as I did, and he didn't understand why I was being treated this way. He spoke up for me and asked, "Why are you being mean to Veronica when all she's done is come in with a smile saying good morning, and she's just trying to learn? We've been in the field for more than ten years, and if we don't want to help her, shame on us." I'm glad my friend stood up for me because I probably would have left the clinic that day since I felt completely shocked by this behavior.

Build Relationships with Colleagues

You need people in your work life to help support you. You need to have people in your corner to vouch for who you really are as a person. You need to have support from all areas to move up and stay on the top. I gain respect from my peers by showing them respect as key contributors to any project we are all equally involved in. You cannot finish a project or achieve anything without people backing you, sharing their ideas, and helping you complete it. You may get it done alone, and it could take longer, but wouldn't it have been more fun with other people who were service line experts in their field? Not to mention that working as a team improves the process and the project quality since one person can't think of everything.

When you're building relationships with colleagues, you get to create a great networking circle. Being in the same career field, you find people with common interests. My friend "O" is a COO in his company and is on track to be the next CEO. My friend "R" is with the health system next door and is on track to be the next COO. My friend "S" was the CEO of a large health system, took a break after the pandemic to do consulting work, and is now on the C-suite track again. We are all at different stages in our lives, but having genuine connections that can lend an ear when we need a confidence boost is extremely comforting. In our careers, most healthcare executives, at some point, know each other or know of each other because everyone has been part of different health systems at one time or another. We are not just competing with each other; we are also helping one another by sharing our best ideas to improve our field.

If you were to ask my friends or professors what they thought about my networking skills, they would most likely rate me on the low end of the scale. I didn't realize how important networking is. Surrounding yourself with like-minded individuals who share similar goals is important because the struggles you are experiencing are most likely struggles they have been through or will go through. They know what opportunities are out there if you are looking for a job. They also are a great resource to draw on by asking about what organizations they have experienced that would match their vision with your core values.

Having a great network takes time, so don't rush into wanting to meet everyone who's influential in your career field. Genuine connections are the ones that will last the longest and help you the most. Get involved in the local chapters of any organization that fills your needs. Get involved in community outreach projects if you want to meet purpose-filled individuals. Get involved in your organization's events to build relationships outside your department. There are so many avenues you can use to build your network. You would be surprised how many people want to help others.

Mentor

Look out for potential mentorship opportunities to build your skill sets. At one point during my C-Suite tenure I was thinking about leaving my job because I wanted to continue growing to oversee hospital operations. I was trying to figure out which was the best healthcare organization for me, one with some leadership opportunities where I could grow. I reached out to one of our executives and let her know how I felt and why. She had trained in other organizations and was willing to take time out of her busy schedule to teach me. I never thought she would take me under her wing and help me strengthen my skills. If there isn't a mentorship program in your organization, reach out to others who are more seasoned to bounce your ideas off. You never know who is willing to give you that time because they see a potential in you that you may not see as clearly in yourself.

Informal mentors are, to me, the best because they grow completely organically. I've had the privilege to work alongside a few mentors that I think the world of. It's completely different guidance when it comes from experienced individuals in your career who want to help you because they actually care about you. My experience with informal mentors has been tremendously game-changing when it comes to believing in myself. You create a bond where there is mutual respect, and you both root for each other to succeed. Being able to build these relationships has helped me navigate political waters, evaluate my decision-making process, and reassess my assumptions about situations.

Potential mentorship opportunities are not always to gain knowledge or feedback from people who have more experience than you. Reverse mentoring can provide valuable lessons from someone with less experience who is in a different age bracket. These individuals often have a different mindset and outlook on the world. Reverse mentoring has completely opened my eyes to how I navigate or lead others in the younger generation. I have had interns from whom I have learned different strategies for developing relationships. I also gained insights into what motivates people to want to do more in their current job roles.

I had an intern with a lot of potential, and I met with him every other week to go over projects that we had developed together to help him grow into the leader he wanted to become. Seeing his confidence grow and seeing him build relationships has really filled my heart, and I've learned from seeing him navigate through waters differently than I do. He analyzes projects from start to finish and evaluates all possible outcomes before making decisions to ensure they make the most sense.

Build up Your Team

I've encountered leaders who don't acknowledge their team or want them to learn more. They are great at what they do, and they want to keep them in the same role forever. That's not realistic. When you build up your team, you're able to evaluate what strengths and weaknesses everyone has. I evaluate the team annually to figure out if we need to add someone else with a different skill set to strengthen the team and close any gaps. As the fastest-growing department in our organization, we are always looking to be innovative, and sometimes, that means adding something completely different to our workflows.

Having a strong support system of team members and processes is crucial to your development as a leader. Trusting that if you go on vacation, someone will attend a meeting for you and report back can really bring peace of mind. There should always be at least one person who knows what's going on and can speak on topics when you're not around. Figure out what strengths your team has and develop them. When you have a great team, you look good.

Your success will be partly due to your support team. Delegate tasks and projects that build on their strengths. Figure out their goals and ambitions. Is there a position that they can move up to one day? Is this a stepping stone to move them up again in a year or two? After you learn more about the person's ambitions, you can create more impactful projects and know they will enjoy them because it gets them closer to reaching their goal. You'd be surprised how much better people do when they actually want to do it. Once you figure out what their goals are, you will also figure out what you cannot give them.

Focus on individuals who are passionate about the organization's vision, whether they are lifelong employees or using their position as a stepping stone to move up or out of the organization, and help them grow into roles that are mutually beneficial. Always think about how you can maximize people's strengths, even if they only give you a year or two. Figure out how they can all work together and who can take what piece of a project. When you know everyone's strengths and goals, you can figure out who can take tasks off your plate.

Let people be who they want to be. There are so many personality types, and it is important to give everyone the opportunity to play to their strengths. Who is the know-it-all on your team that wants to know everything? Let them. Make them the resource that people can go to and ask questions. Let them be who they want to be, and if that's a know-it-all, then give them something to help the entire team move with a project. Do you have someone who is always playing devil's advocate? You need someone who thinks about the pros and cons in every situation to alleviate potential mistakes when implementing a new change. Or you may have a person on your team who just doesn't trust anyone and tells you why. That's okay. Maybe this person can audit the project because you need someone to see what kinks or areas have been missed.

If you are a current leader and want to grow, you need to keep succession planning in the back of your mind. And while building up your team, this is a perfect opportunity for you to learn who wants your role next and see if they are coachable.

Make Genuine Connections at Work

You will be happier having a support system at work. I always tell my team to vent to each other when it comes to things that are out of their control. And I tell them to vent to each other because who wants to go home and talk about work? The people and/or fur babies at home don't understand your struggles because they don't work with you. It's great to have that support system with your peers because they may have gone through the same situation a year ago and can tell you how they fixed it.

Stress from work shouldn't be taken home because people in your household will unfortunately not be able to solve your problems. Having that support system at work really helps you get out of your funk quicker. The way that I de-stress at work is by singing or cracking jokes with my right-hand staffer. I laugh at myself more than anything else, and that de-stresses me.

If you have genuine connections at work, you're able to have that safe zone where you can let it out. You will be happier when you have that because you're not internalizing all your feelings and digging yourself into a rabbit hole about something that could be solved by just talking to someone. When you're making genuine connections at work, you'll be able to gather more ideas by talking to like-minded individuals who share the same love in your career field.

I told a good friend that our directors were having a one-hour book club on leadership, and we would discuss it and talk about our feelings. Out of that conversation, he took it upon himself to get the book and do the same exercise with his team, and that really helped them build more group cohesiveness with some structure behind it, where people were not just venting. It helped both our teams have an open space and build stronger, genuine connections. If you don't have strong relationships, you can't get the best out of what other people are doing. Having these connections or relationships at work will make you more motivated to do great things together. By having connections with my peers who have the same mindset and career level as me, we tend to push each other to want to do more, to collaborate with each other, and to speak at conferences. You never know who is going to help you the most in the relationships that you've built with different peers at your workplace.

Build relationships with your bosses where there is open discussion with feedback to do better, not just for yourself, but for the department and the organization that you work for. I've seen this time and time again where young professionals feel a particular way, and it's easier to just talk to everyone else about their boss than to have a frank discussion with them.

Here's my advice:

1. **Don't talk about your boss negatively to your co-workers.** If you have a valid issue with them, bring it up with your boss or your human resources department. Your boss will find out. It's happened, and I've seen it. We're all human; if you have an issue, speak with that person that you have an issue with because it may have all been fabricated in your head. When you start speaking about your boss, you could be labeled as a complainer. You may have only done it one time, but sometimes, that's all it takes to change people's perception of who you are. It can make it seem like you don't have the confidence and self-worth to resolve your issue with your boss on your own.

2. **Ask what other projects your boss needs help with.** Most bosses enjoy it when you take the initiative to help take something off their plate. This really shows them that this is not just

a job for you. I appreciate being asked if there are additional projects my direct reports can help me with because it makes it easier to delegate tasks.

3. **Worry about what your boss thinks, not the rest of the crowd.** A friend of mine had an individual wanting to move up, so he gave her the chance to be in the spotlight and go to meetings with him. His employee started doing things for other departments instead of doing what he had asked her to do. My advice to him was that he needed to make the roles and responsibilities of her job clear while still letting her know he supported her in building those relationships with other departments, but with set deadlines and clear expectations. Seriously, worry about what your boss thinks first because that is the person that you report to. Instead of trying to please everyone, you need to know how to prioritize what's important, what can wait, and what is definitely not for today. Remember, your evaluation is done by your boss, so start there and shine bright!

4. **Feedback is extremely important.** If your boss is giving you constructive criticism, it's because either they are seeing an issue or your peers are seeing it. They are trying to help you without hurting your feelings. Young leaders or new careerists tend to get very defensive when a leader is trying to correct a behavior or really giving them a heads-up. It could be because they have gotten that feedback before about themselves and don't want you to make the same mistakes. Listen to what they

tell you to fix because it may not be something wrong in your eyes, but you may be coming across as unapproachable.

My master's program taught me a lot about networking and having genuine relationships to help each other out. I refuse to believe everyone is always trying to wish you harm or trying to cut you down. I surround myself with people who prove to me their real selves through their actions. If you can't trust others, it will be very difficult to stay focused on accomplishing your goals.

CHAPTER 7

You Have to Fail to Succeed

A lot of young professionals try to be perfect, always say the right thing, and never make a mistake. It makes me wonder why. Then I think back and ask myself, *Was I trying to connect to, adapt to, or become someone I thought my superiors wanted me to be?* If you are climbing the career ladder right now, your boss knows you will make a mistake. We usually put more pressure on ourselves than we actually need to. When we feel we have to act a certain way or we don't want to make a mistake because we want someone to see the best in us, we don't realize we could be hurting our own career growth. Do you want to complete a project on time and be called out for a few mistakes, or do you want to perfect the project in a year when the due date is in one month?

No one is perfect, and mistakes will happen, but how you deal with your mistakes will define your success. You are expected to complete your assignments, but you are not expected to get them 100 percent perfect on your first attempt. I say this because we can try to do our very best, but there's no need to overanalyze yourself in a way that hinders the completion of the project.

Ask, Ask, and Ask Again

You are expected to meet deadlines, but you are not expected to complete a project without asking for help. When you don't ask questions, it'll be harder for you to know your superior's vision or whoever asked you to complete the project. The one thing that frustrates me the most is when I delegate a project to my team, and they don't ask questions, do not request follow-up meetings to go over the project in detail, or just respond, "Everything is fine," when I ask how it is going. As we approach the deadline for the project, I discover that it has a completely different vision from what I had in mind. This makes it more difficult and frustrates everyone working on it because they now have to go back and redo it.

Dumb questions make you smart. I say this because I don't believe there are dumb questions. I believe there are only questions. Whether it's something that someone else knew or if it's something that no one knew, it's great to ask a question because you never know what you're going to get out of that. You may learn something new. You may have something to add while you are getting clarification. And when you ask a question that you need clarification on, that 10-second question may save you an hour wondering about it.

When I worked in another department of the health system I currently work for, I would often sit in on meetings where I had no clue what they were talking about. During the meeting, I would write words or phrases down that I didn't understand, so I could ask the subject expert to explain. If it was just a question, I could ask them when we were walking out of the meeting. But if it was a process that I knew probably would take more time, I would ask them if they could sit with me for a few minutes to explain it. They never said no. Most people want to help others understand and some people actually like it when people are interested in what they know so they can explain it. Keep an eye on the people who really enjoy teaching so they can be your go-to people if you feel comfortable asking even the simplest questions.

There's a difference between being dumb and asking dumb questions. I think it's something that we all struggle with. I recently was talking to an audience member who is actually one of our trusted partners, and they asked me to talk to their employees about leadership and some topics on emotional intelligence. They asked, "How do you ask your boss a dumb question without them thinking that you are dumb or that you don't know what you're doing?" That struck a chord with me because I prefer to have an open-door culture where there is no dumb question and learning is accepted and welcomed. I told that individual that asking questions and genuinely being interested in learning more would make you stand out. In my experience, people that ask questions are engaged. They actually want to know how they're doing in their workplace, want to learn more, and are people I think of when a management position opens up.

Take Chances on Initiatives That May or May Not Succeed

During COVID, the culture in our organization changed. We had to think differently, act faster, make on-the-spot decisions, and figure out how to tweak them. Were there mistakes that happened along the way when we had to change processes to get our patients into our facilities as quickly as possible so they weren't waiting in the lobby? Absolutely. Was it life-threatening or something we couldn't fix? Absolutely not. If we had not taken the chance to implement a process, there could have been X, Y, and Z factors that fortunately didn't happen. Our providers could see patients that needed to be seen. We implemented a telemedicine platform, where we had to add another workflow to the clinic during the COVID chaos. It took some brainstorming, getting people together, using cell phones at first, then tablets/computers, and we finally were able to get on one platform and educate our 200 providers in 75 locations.

There were a ton of mistakes, but the fastest way to tweak the process was to learn from our mistakes instead of brainstorming every possible mistake before implementing a process we had no experience with. Don't be so worried about failure because failure can make you more successful if you learn from your mistakes. If you are like some people I know who can't accept failure, then you will take a longer time moving on to the next best thing in your future.

Being one innovator in our health system, we implemented a successful virtual workforce, which we have completely changed both on-site and in another country where they performed administrative tasks that we didn't necessarily have to do in person. This worked well in some locations but not so well in others, which was mostly due to a lack of buy-in and not being open-minded about changing. We had thought the virtual workforce could work in any of our clinic locations, but not all managers worked the same or had the same experience level. We had to slow down and iron out kinks with the management team that we usually used to pilot most of our projects.

Without implementing or joining forces with our virtual workforce company, we would have had to close some clinics due to limited resources. The workforce has completely changed over the years. This project has given our local team some friendly competition on the hybrid departments that work with local and out-of-country staff. Even though it was tough at first to prove that having a hybrid workforce is the future, we kept fighting with data on all the benefits it gave us in our department.

There will be projects that are a bust. Learn when to close them out and move on to the next best thing. Don't let your ego get in the way of your success. Not everything is going to go the way you planned as you are dealing with people who don't think the way you do. Don't lose your cool, and don't get disappointed. Some things will be wins, and a lot will be losses. Unfortunately, we tend to focus on the losses to define us instead of just learning from them and brushing them off. Try to master this art of letting go as fast as possible.

Take Chances on People That May or May Not Succeed

We sometimes hire people who may think and act like we do. Sometimes, you need to have a different personality or an expert in a different field, even though you may think it might not work. These individuals may be the ones that really surprise you and work the best with you because they think differently. Leading a team will always have ups and downs, especially because the hardest thing is dealing with people. I think it's the most rewarding when you're able to help others, but it has been the most disappointing when you trust someone and they take advantage of your kindness. This will happen. It's human nature. Does it hurt? Yes. But will I change the way I treat people? No. I think most people are good and want to do the right thing.

As a leader, I like to encourage my direct reports to create a culture where mistakes are lessons learned instead of being thought of as just a chance to dish out punishments, write-ups, and discipline. If we create that culture of fear, then there will be people who won't mention their mistakes when they should or won't volunteer for a project because it's not fulfilling, not fun, more work, and it's not enjoyable. If you are a leader, encourage and support your team to move on and learn from their failures. It gives people that space to create. It gives people the freedom to think independently. It gives people the happiness they need to innovate. There's obviously a thin line between mistakes that you didn't anticipate and mistakes that are careless because of lazy work. So, you should try to create a culture where mistakes are lessons learned but don't create a culture where mistakes are excuses for them not doing the best work they can. There's a thin line when it comes to that.

Over the years, I realized that people's feedback about others may be factual but doesn't define their entire character as an individual. A friend of mine was on the fence about hiring an individual from another department because he'd heard this individual was intelligent but didn't close the loop on projects timely, thought very highly of themselves, and was not an early bird. My advice to him was that if he thought they were a great fit in everything else, he should take the chance and just closely monitor those opportunities for improvement. You will never find the perfect candidate that can do it all. You have to figure out if the pros outweigh the cons because everyone has both. The feedback that was given was actually true about the individual, but it was because the individual wanted to take on all projects, would stay late most days, and had the confidence to speak to others about what needed to be done.

When Mistakes Happen, Reflect on That Failure to Move Forward

Learn to accept failure when your idea doesn't work. It will happen. Move on and regroup. We can tend to get stuck wondering why an idea didn't work. Why is no one embracing this implementation? Why can't we try it again for the 10th time? Because it probably won't work the 11th time. These are five questions that I ask myself when something goes wrong or when something could go better.

- Was there a particular function that didn't work as planned?
- Was there an adoption problem?
- Did you have the right people giving you input?

- What knowledge and experience did you gain from this?
- What are you going to do now to prevent this from happening again?

Always remember that the faster you move forward from your failures, the easier it is to get out of your funk.

I had a great relationship with a coworker whom I had moved up within the ranks of the department that I now oversee. Out of the blue, I got a call from a different department asking me if I wanted to strip her access—to the building, computer, etc. I asked them why I would want to do that, and they told me she'd left. She'd quit. I wondered how they knew that before me, given she was working for me. So, I opened my computer, and sure enough, she had sent her resignation email to me and my HR director late at night when I was at a board meeting. I was in complete shock, but I had to move on and consider who would oversee her team.

Fairly quickly, I promoted someone from within and gave them a chance to see how they could lead this team. I did not think that someone so close to me that I trusted would do something like that, but you don't know what's going on in someone's mind unless they feel comfortable enough to tell you.

As a result, I considered what I could do better to prevent this from happening to someone else. Did I place too much pressure on the team? Did I need to have check-ins with the team about how they were doing? A couple of years later, she reached out to me when I was on vacation with my mom and wished me a happy birthday. I thanked her and wished her well. I think that goes to show that maybe something was going on in her personal life, or maybe I overwhelmed her with so many projects because I depended on her so much. I will probably never know the real reason behind her decision, but it made me more cautious about how many duties I placed on individuals. People won't usually tell you they're overwhelmed as they don't want to disappoint you. Most people want to figure it out on their own, but it may be a lot faster when they have guidance early on. I always try to end my meetings with, "Is there anything I can do to help?" but even this may not be enough for your overachievers.

Prioritizing the list of what needs to be done yesterday, tomorrow, next week, or next year helps when giving directions and expectations. During COVID, I learned the need to slow down and focus on safety first, the quality and mental health of our team, and the basics of doing our jobs. Once things stabilized and we had a better mindset, we started creating again. I learned to take a step back and analyze what was really important, what could wait, and what did and didn't make sense.

There are pros and cons to being a trailblazer. If you implement things too fast, there will be more mistakes. If you take a little more time and talk to others, there are still going to be mistakes, but hopefully fewer, and they can be fixed along the way. I have always looked for the next best thing to help our department run smoothly, but now I keep in mind the limited resources I have to implement something.

Your Leadership Style Has to Be Constantly Tweaked

You can't win if you have never failed. You can't be a better leader if you have never learned what you need to get better at. The first few times I got feedback, I was internally devastated. I felt like I had done my best, but it still wasn't good enough. I quickly realized this feedback was critical for my success as a leader. It isn't what you think you do but what your team perceives you to do. It is good to learn from a great leader, but you will most likely have different personalities on your team, which in turn creates different scenarios that you have to deal with.

Top 10 Leadership Tips

1. Don't be on your phone or computer while your direct report is meeting with you.

2. Don't talk about your superior in a negative light to your direct reports.

3. Don't get frustrated when your direct report takes longer to understand a process.

4. Over-communicate everything that is extremely important.

5. Don't be so quick to take a side when you have only heard one side of the story.

6. Don't hold grudges against employees who provide feedback.

7. Don't intentionally embarrass your direct report in front of their peers.

8. Don't pretend to know the answer to everything your direct report asks.

9. Don't promise things that you have no authority or control over.

10. Analyze the feedback you receive; some may be just opinions of their reality.

CHAPTER 8

Stop Doubting Yourself

Moving up the career ladder, you will doubt yourself over and over again. You will ask yourself, *Am I a good leader? Why didn't I know how to answer that question? I need to work long hours and weekends to prove that I'm committed. How do I prioritize my time to be able to serve everyone equally?* People you surround yourself with will constantly tell you how good you are, but you are the only one who needs to believe you are good enough to succeed.

Break Your Internal Barriers

What if I had done this? What if I had applied here instead of here? What if I had taken this job? Those internal barriers are just distractions in your head about something that is in the past that you should not be focused on because it's now over. I had a moment in my career recently where I lost focus on my purpose. I was burned out, and I was upset at a choice that had nothing to do with me, but I felt like my competence was being questioned. I stopped thinking about what the team needed, and I started thinking of what I needed, which didn't align with my core values. I went down a rabbit hole. It took time for me to get grounded again and focus on what made me happy going to work every day.

Most of our self-doubt is absolute nonsense and just fog that doesn't allow us to think clearly. The best way to break your internal barriers is to talk about them with yourself and with people who know and care about you. A friend didn't understand why she had done so badly on her evaluation, which meant she did not get a bonus. She was so down on herself that she could only talk about what her boss thought of her. I asked her what advice her boss had given her to improve. She then realized she hadn't spoken to him about the evaluation, and she had not even seen it. She got up the courage to set up a meeting with him to understand what grade she had received and why. He didn't understand the reason for the meeting, as he thought he had given her an above-average evaluation. However, when he checked his system, he realized he hadn't graded her yet that year, which was why she hadn't received her bonus. He told her that next time, she was to check with him instead of wasting time doubting her capabilities. She was embarrassed at what had happened and mad at herself for ever thinking she was not doing a good job. She was actually graded one of the highest among her peers.

When trying to break down internal barriers, keep these five things in the back of your mind.

1. Someone else's opinion about you is just an opinion, so brush it off.

2. Nobody knows everything about everything, so relax.

3. What is for you will be for you; let go of what isn't for you.

4. You only know how much you can handle at one time that will not physically and mentally break you, so listen to your mind and soul.

5. We all have a purpose in life, so stay focused on achieving it.

Don't Underestimate Your Worth

My friend was just about to accept her promotion but was terrified that she would have to deal with more egotistical men and women who thought they knew it all. She knew she could do the job, but she didn't know how she would navigate work politics, as she had heard horror stories from her boss. She would now have to take the calls her boss used to take, and some weren't that nice. She had heard her boss getting screamed at through the wall separating their offices, and she cringed at the thought of those calls coming to her. She ran through what she would talk about or how she would answer questions when asked.

There have been so many scenarios where I have caught myself thinking, *Wow, that's a new one I haven't heard before. You can't make this up.* Colleagues have also reported having experiences they never thought would happen in their work life. As much as you want to know how to handle situations, there are times that you won't know how to handle the situation, and you're just going to have to take a step back and say, *Are they really talking to me when they're screaming at me about a process that I had nothing to do with? Is this reflecting on me, or is this something I need to fix so I'm glad to learn about it?*

My friend ended up getting her promotion and started getting a call from one of the executives. That call was to ask questions he knew she wouldn't be able to answer off the top of her head. There were numerous calls. So, she felt even more defeated in the sense that there was no way that she could memorize whatever answer to the question he had. So, she ended up deciding to say, "I don't know right now, but let me get back to you." This irritated the executive, and more questions came about why she didn't know the answers.

Thankfully, she had a mentor in the same profession as the executive, and he advised her that it was a form of bullying and that the only way to stop a bully was by confronting them. Human resources helped her have a conversation with the executive about the reason for the calls. He was asked to reply in writing, but they determined there was no need for the executive to call her because she didn't report to him. He had nothing to do with her department. She doesn't understand why the executive targeted her and made her feel like she was not good enough.

She doubted herself and her worth, but her mentor said, "You have done more for this department in one year than any of your predecessors have." She already knew this, but her mindset was clouded because of this one individual. No one should have that much control over your emotions to make you feel less important.

Don't Underestimate Your Strength and Influence

I recently visited friends in a different part of the world who thought I was perfect. I couldn't understand why. I knew I was not perfect, but I wondered why they saw me in this light. I was on holiday and in a calm, stress-free state of mind with no worries about real life and all the responsibilities that I had at home. And it made me realize I needed this state of inner peace to be the best version of myself at work and in my day-to-day life because that was my strength. If people saw me as their definition of perfect, then that's what I wanted to shoot for and be the best version of myself in all aspects of my life.

We tend not to realize that others look at us for advice or to see what we've done on social media, in our titles, or other accomplishments we have obtained. It is true when people say you may leave a mark on someone you spoke to once. A front-line person who is now on our management team pulled me aside at our Christmas manager's party and said, "Five years ago, I asked you how you moved up so quickly. I've always admired your presence and your overall 'nice' energy. I told myself I was going to move up and then tell you that you are an example of the type of leader I wanted to be." I try to always be on my A-game at work, even when I'm mentally exhausted and don't have the energy to carry on a conversation. You never know who you are inspiring or who needs a little motivation to make it through the day. Kindness should always be at the forefront.

You Don't Know What You Don't Know

I've seen my colleagues get in their heads and wonder if they're good enough. Maybe because of this, you think you don't know as much as you do. You do know as much as you do. There are things that will not work. We are human; we aren't perfect. And the faster you move on from your idea that didn't work and regroup and find another solution, the easier it'll be in your life and also your team's life.

It's great to know that you care about being better, but it's not okay for you to think you're not good enough for the role that you have been given because there was at least one person who believed that you could do the role and wants you to succeed. You know what you know, and you don't know what you don't know, and that's okay.

If All Else Fails, Leave

Do not stay in a position where you feel stuck because, most likely, you are. And then, if you're not comfortable with the job, you can always go to a job that you are comfortable with. So, I'm going to give you a few tips on how to do this. The first thing to do is weigh out your pros and cons. We're not working late hours because we're comfortable and know what we're doing. But when you want to grow, that may be the only time to read up on what you need to learn to be comfortable in your role. Do you want to grow in your position to have a bigger impact? Or do you want to enjoy life traveling so you're okay with where you are?

Are you in an environment where you've tapped out and hit a glass ceiling? It all depends on what you are looking for in your future. If you're okay with your job for the next X years because you want to do something else that will take up your time, then do that. If you're in a job where there's no room to grow, start looking or asking your boss if there's an additional project for you or if they can keep you in mind for growth opportunities. You need to weigh up your pros and cons because sometimes we have this perception where when you're writing it down on paper, you don't realize all the pros that you may be able to leverage to say, *Okay, I am still growing because I have [X, Y, and Z] at my workplace.* Or when you're writing down your cons, you can say to yourself, *I have [X, Y, and Z], and there's no more room to grow here.* I believe in loyalty because that is one of my values, but you need to have more loyalty to yourself and your family than a job. A job is a job, and it's great to be loyal to the company, which I think is very important just for your own state of happiness, but you also have to do what's best for you.

When you're moving up the career ladder in the same organization, you may end up supervising your friends who were your co-workers. You will start freaking out about how you will navigate being their boss and their friend outside of work. One of the common mistakes I have made with managers or shining stars that move up is how I draw the line between friendship and managing the staff professionally. I had a friend stepping into her role who already knew the team she would oversee. She quickly realized that once she was their boss, they treated her differently. They didn't include her in some of the lunches that they would have previously and in some of their conversations. She started seeing them in a different light from a supervisor's perspective, a different dynamic she hadn't seen when they were just peers. So, my advice is to take off your blinders and see people for who they are and what they show you at work. Evaluate if they are the right cultural fit.

Once, I had a direct report whose behavior was unacceptable. I had to make an executive decision to let her go, even though she was great at what she did. I couldn't have that type of personality or leader on the team because we were working so hard to change the work environment into a servant leadership culture of empowerment. It affected me because I try to give people the benefit of the doubt. I send out communications that I have an open-door policy to eliminate these types of direct reports and perceptions that are hurting our culture more than helping.

Take Chances on Yourself to Learn Something New

I was so excited to expand and share my knowledge that I applied to numerous conferences as a speaker—and I was accepted to all of them. It was very hard for me to juggle all of them simultaneously because I was speaking at a conference and on a podcast (which goes back to when to say no to things), and I was asked to contribute to medical journals. I was then asked to be on the board for the following year's conference and to speak to other committees and companies. It's been a source of great pride for me to take up these opportunities, but it has also shown me what I need to work on when I'm speaking at a conference—such as who my audience is—with the feedback that I received at each speaking event, which is always great.

Truth hurts sometimes, but you have to take it as a learning lesson and not focus on the one negative comment from someone who didn't like your presentation. Yes, read the feedback and see how you can do better, but don't let it discourage you. Don't quit, and don't let someone's random opinion of you overpower your accomplishments or how you see yourself. When you're trying or learning something new, you're not always going to get it right the first time. Everyone says practice makes perfect, so keep practicing, and you'll make fewer mistakes.

CHAPTER 9

The Reality of Being in the C-Suite at Age 30

I've Learned That You Do Not Need to Prove Your Point in Every Meeting

I used to be someone who wanted to correct everyone's perception of reality, which often placed me in challenging situations. There is a time and place to prove your point, but interrupting meetings with no data to prove your point is unnecessary and doesn't respect other people's time—especially where an agenda is set, and there is no time left to open up the meeting for questions or feedback. I quickly realized that when I was trying to prove my point, it became a 30-minute discussion that could have been taken offline in a smaller setting with the appropriate parties involved. You do not want to get the reputation of being the annoying person who just wants to hear themselves talk. Try listening more when it's not a meeting you coordinated but were just invited to. Most of the time, your questions will be answered by the end of the meeting.

If you are thinking about asking a question, ask yourself if this is something that will take more than five minutes to solve. If it is, wait till the end and ask if there's time. If there's not enough time, pull that person aside so you can let them know what you want them to know, and always think about the point you are trying to prove. Is that the right forum to prove it, or will you just confuse everyone because no one knows what you're talking about? Don't get me wrong, always speak up if you have something to add that everyone needs to know about, but try to reserve your energy if you truly know that it will either confuse your audience or waste their time.

I've Learned People Believe What They Want to Believe, and It Is Just Easier to Prove Them Wrong With Your Success

Our department was the red-headed stepchild of the entire company, or so we thought. The executive team would talk about how the department needed policies and procedures in place. Our department is now one of the most innovative departments in our company. The team is much more cohesive, as we all share the same passion for improving. We share our processes so others don't have to recreate the wheel. We stay focused on our vision to improve our department. We went through many rough patches together, which has made us appreciate each other and be more tolerant of whatever comes our way. We wouldn't have gotten to where we are now if we had kept the same victim mentality that we were the most poorly run department.

We do get in our funks when we feel like all we are receiving is negative feedback, but we try to get out of them quickly. My competitive mindset kicks in, and we start thinking of all the options we have to solve our problems. I have learned that negative mindsets are a waste of time and energy. We wouldn't be able to introduce new processes to the organization if we stayed worried about what others were thinking. Remember, everyone has an opinion. It's how you navigate those opinions—good and bad—that will make you stand out from the crowd.

I've Learned That There Are Many Insecure People Who Would Rather Focus On Others' Faults Than Better Themselves

Don't be one of these people. I was having a conversation with one of my mentors, and he was telling me how proud he was of my growth, how much I've worked on getting where I am, and how I have been able to gain the respect of his peers. It was great to hear, but he ended the conversation by saying that it would, unfortunately, cause many to envy me. This harsh reality was a good warning for me to be cautious and not such an open book about things no one needs to know about. Being too vulnerable can make someone twist your words into an insecurity that you never thought you had.

It's easier to just envy someone than to actually understand them for who they truly are and what they've had to overcome to get to where they're at. It used to make me extremely sad to know people would talk about me, but then I realized these individuals didn't know I'd worked countless hours to learn every role I was in and had shed many tears of frustration when I did not understand something. I know I'm not the most intelligent or the most polished. My Spanglish comes out on most days when I run out of English words to say. But there isn't one day that I sulk and think about other people's accomplishments because I'm focusing on mine and how to better serve my team.

I've Learned to Adapt to Personalities and Understand That Everyone Has Their Own Agendas

Everyone has a different purpose in life. Some of your peers are only in their role because of how much money they are making. Some of your peers want more power so they can secure their position in the company. Some of your peers are "yes people" who only want to please those they think are important instead of focusing on the success of the organization. Some of your peers are so lost that they try to stay silent so they won't be called out for not understanding their own role. Some of your peers have been in their roles for so long that they are comfortable and seek to minimize change, so they don't have to work as hard as they did in their earlier years. Some of your peers are just waiting to get a better opportunity in another organization.

Once you start realizing that none of this matters to your success when you are in the C-suite, you will be much happier. You can't change anyone's mindset except your own. Once you understand people's personal agendas at work, you can place yourself in their shoes and figure out why they talked to you in a certain way and let it roll off your back. It is also an advantage because you will know who will shut down your ideas because they don't align with their needs and who you need to influence to help you push your ideas through. Adapting to personalities and understanding why people do what they do will help you navigate the C-suite a lot better.

I've Learned Not to Judge People Without Getting to Know Them

When I start to judge others, I always remember this saying from one of my mentors: "There is only one judge (higher being), and that is not me." It helps me stay in my soft women era. No one will be exactly like you, but that doesn't mean that they are a bad person. There are some individuals who feel like they have to act a certain way or belittle people to show that they have authority, which I don't agree with, but that is something that they may have been trained to do by their old bosses. There are some individuals who may lie because they don't want you to know that they need help due to fear of losing their job.

I used to let others' perceptions of an individual influence my thoughts. I stopped this behavior after meeting one of my closest friends at work. I had already decided I wasn't going to trust him because of who I thought he surrounded himself with. We ended up working together, but not by choice, which was the best thing that could have happened to me. Make your own decisions about people. Consider the source that is talking to you about a certain individual. They might have issues with everyone because they may be the common denominator causing the drama. Most of us believe that actions speak louder than words, so why do we allow the words of others to influence our perception of someone? Even if I end up getting burned by a person the same way I was told I would, I feel better knowing I ended up forming my own conclusions about them with my own experiences.

I've Learned My Struggles at Work Are Shared With Others Going through the Same Thoughts, Feelings, and Expectations

We sometimes believe that no one else just got punched in the gut by criticism or was given a deadline with a two-day notice to complete. Reality check: You aren't that special. Take a step back and look around to see who else is being asked for items to be completed at lightning speed. You would be surprised to know that most are in the same boat. Once you have a circle of close peers with whom you can take a lunch break to clear your mind, it makes work life so much more enjoyable and sometimes helps you find solutions to your issues from a different point of view.

The younger you are, the less experience you have and the more barriers you will have to overcome, and it's okay if you learn how to navigate these issues and not go into a rabbit hole. Having feelings about something you are passionate about is completely normal. Getting so involved in your feelings that you start thinking negatively about every scenario is not normal. Learn to let go of things that are out of your control, which includes others' misperceptions about you. You can only do as much as you are capable of doing.

I've Learned to Be a Better Leader Through My Team

You will never be a perfect leader, so don't strive for perfection. That doesn't exist. Just like social media, everyone has an opinion, even if you thought you'd covered all bases to try to be fair to all. The longer you work with people, the more they understand you as a person. The team is now comfortable telling me what I need to improve and what I need to keep doing. The worst experiences you have had when having to lead a team are the experiences that will mold you into a better leader. It doesn't matter how many leadership books you read or how many podcasts you listen to; making mistakes and owning up to those perceptions that your team has of you is the only thing that can make you a better leader. Next time you waste your time listening to someone give an opinion about leading, ask your team what you can improve.

I now oversee many teams, which makes it hard for me to connect as much as I would like to due to having such a tight schedule. Back when I only had a handful of direct reports, I knew every milestone and every heartache each of them was going through, from grandkids to having kids, to divorce, to marriage. Being in the C-suite, I've learned that getting to know all my direct reports at that personal level was impossible. It didn't mean that I didn't care about them as much. It just meant I had to think about the well-being of the entire department. I've acknowledged that I won't be everyone's cup of tea. I've acknowledged that the way I speak may unintentionally offend someone, and genuinely apologizing for the miscommunication is key to moving on. I've acknowledged that I do not always have the best judgment when hiring new team members, which is why I do not interview candidates on my own. I've acknowledged that I'm way too lenient on people because I truly see the best in them, even though they have shown their true colors in time. I've acknowledged that I will always need to improve my leadership style, and that's okay.

I've Learned That It Is Okay to Place Boundaries on My Own Definition of a Work-Life Balance

As I mentioned, it's hard for me to say no to things, especially if I know I have the time but may not have the energy for it. I have good boundaries about not answering calls and texts when I get home from work or when I'm on vacation. I still remember when I was with my mom in Italy on a museum tour. I was so focused on what our guide was telling us. All of a sudden, I got a text from a physician asking me to please give them a call. A two-minute conversation turned into a 15-minute conversation, and I missed that time with my mom about paintings we really enjoyed. It was an issue that I could have addressed when I got back. I told myself I would never put myself in a situation like that where I would regret a memory with my loved ones. Thankfully, I was able to go back to that museum and fully understand the meaning of those paintings just last year.

Sadly, I see people sacrifice what they love to do because they have this idea that they don't belong and have to prove themselves. People who are not in your position will always talk, positive or negative, so if they have no influence on you obtaining a raise or a promotion, why are you spending your energy trying to please them? My outlet to recharge is traveling the world as much as possible. It keeps me grounded about what reality is in the world and not what I think reality is in my own little world at work. Whatever your outlet is to recharge, learn to be consistent with it so you won't get in funks. Trust me, nobody wants to deal with a leader who is always in a bad mood because they are in a mentally bad cycle.

I've Learned That You Need to Appreciate Yourself and Not Expect Anyone Else To

The reinforcement that you're doing a great job was not something I craved because I kept getting promoted pretty quickly, which was appreciation enough for me. We all want to be appreciated for our work, but you aren't going to hear you are doing a great job every day because the perception is that you have to be somewhat good to be in the C-suite. It not only gets lonely at the top because few people know the struggles you have to deal with, but it is also exhausting trying to be enough for everyone, including yourself. Most of the time, it is a thankless job. You have to learn that your job is not to get praise but to give praise and solve as many problems as possible to please the company's clients, stakeholders, and staff.

You have to be mentally strong to take criticism from all levels and not let it deter you from your path to success. I have seen the pressure get to many of my colleagues, but also experienced C-suite leaders who get so wrapped up in trying to be noticed by the most important person in the room instead of focusing on their role to push their department to be stronger and more efficient each year. Don't do things to please others; do them because you think that is the best decision for the organization. If you want to obtain a goal, do it because you believe that is the goal your team needs to be focused on getting to the next level, not because you want to please an individual or a handful of stakeholders. If you feel you need appreciation or validation from others, you're never going to be happy with what you actually bring to the table.

I've Learned Not to Take Things Personally

Unless you own the company, it is just a job, not your life. Your title should never define you. You do what you can with what you have, and tomorrow is another day. If I'm doing the right thing with conviction, that's enough for me to go home and sleep well at night.

If your dream is to get to the C-suite, take your time to understand the responsibility and the sacrifices you will endure. The reality is people will expect a lot from you because they believe you know about every decision the organization makes and are part of it. You are not a taco, so not everyone will like you because the buck stops with you. You will have to make tough decisions and be responsible for them if they don't go to plan. You will need to set expectations and communicate them over and over again. Your priorities are not everyone else's priorities.

The contagious and enjoyable part is you will meet like-minded people who want to collaborate.

You will have more credibility when speaking at conferences or events. You will have the power to help others to fulfill their goals. You will be able to influence others to do the right thing. You will find joy in knowing that every year, there is something new to learn. And this makes it all worth it for me.

I love my job for many reasons. I love that I'm able to create with my team and make things better. I love that I'm able to make changes from a culture of reprimands to a culture of happiness and expression. I love that the people I work for are genuinely good people who try to do their very best every day. I love that I have complete support from my superiors to be able to create and make decisions without any fear of retaliation.

When you get to the C-suite, or whatever your career dream is, use your position for good. There is enough misery and chaos in this world. I truly believe everything happens for a reason. It is up to us to make a positive impact and better the people we are surrounded by.

THANK YOU FOR READING MY BOOK!

For inquiries or mentorship opportunities,
feel free to connect with me on LinkedIn.

Scan the QR Code Here:

I appreciate your interest in my book and value your feedback as it helps me improve future versions of this book. I would appreciate it if you could leave your invaluable review on Amazon.com with your feedback. Thank you!

www.ingramcontent.com/pod-product-compliance
Lightning Source LLC
Chambersburg PA
CBHW020157200326
41521CB00006B/408